WORKS FOR PIANO

Emmanuel Chabrier

EDITED BY
ROY HOWAT

D1604405

DOVER PUBLICATIONS, INC.
New York

Bibliographical Note

This Dover edition, first published in 1995, is a new compilation of music previously published in separate editions. Enoch frères & Costallat, Paris, originally published *Habanera* (1885), *Joyeuse marche* (1890), *Bourrée fantasque* (1891) and *Pièces pittoresques* (1891 and later). Enoch & Cie, Paris, originally published *Cinq pièces* in 1897—comprising *Ronde champêtre*, *Aubade*, *Ballabile*, *Caprice* and *Feuillet d'album*—and *Impromptu*, n.d. *Petite valse*, originally published in *Revue de Musicologie*, vol. 54 (1968), no. 2, pp. 245–6, is reproduced here by the kind authorization of the Société Française de Musicologie.

The Dover edition adds: a unified table of contents, with new English translations of the French titles; a glossary of French terms in the music; and an introduction by editor Roy Howat, written specially for this edition. New French and English headings appear throughout.

Library of Congress Cataloging-in-Publication Data

Chabrier, Emmanuel, 1841–1894.
   [Piano music. Selections]
   Works for piano / Emmanuel Chabrier ; edited by Roy Howat.
     p. of music.
   Reprints of works published in Paris, principally by Enoch, 1885–1897.
   Contents: Impromptu—Ronde champêtre—Petite valse—Pièces pittoresques—Aubade—Habanera—Ballabile—Caprice—Feuillet d'album—Joyeuse marche—Bourrée fantasque.
   ISBN 0-486-28574-X
   1. Piano music. I. Howat, Roy.
M22.C429H68   1995   95-14814
                                                           CIP
                                                               M

Manufactured in the United States of America
Dover Publications, Inc., 31 East 2nd Street, Mineola, N.Y. 11501

Roy Howat is a concert pianist especially known for his expertise in French music. He is also author of the book *Debussy in proportion* and a founding editor of the Paris-based New Complete Debussy Edition (*Oeuvres Complètes de Claude Debussy*). In 1994, he took a major part in Chabrier Centenary Festivals in London and elsewhere; these events resulted in widespread reappraisal of Chabrier's stature. For Editions STIL (Paris), Mr. Howat has recorded Chabrier's piano music, including most of the works in the present volume.

ACKNOWLEDGMENTS

Thanks are expressed to those who kindly made source material available or helped in other ways: Dr. Paul Banks; MM. Thierry Bodin, Denis Herlin, Jean-Michel Nectoux and Alain Planès; Mme. Enoch and Mme. Denis of Enoch & Cie, Paris; Mme. Marie-Noël Colette and the Société Française de Musicologie; Mmes. Marie-France Calas and Fabienne Gaudin, and the staff of the Musée de la Musique, Paris; M. Jacques Tchamkerten and the library of the Geneva Conservatoire; Ms. Margaret Cranmer and the Rowe Music Library, King's College, Cambridge; Ms. Helen Faulkner and the BBC Music Library, London; the music staff of the Bibliothèque Nationale, Paris; the library of the Guildhall School of Music and Drama, London; and especially M. Roger Delage for much vital information and encouragement.

Contents

Glossary of French Terms

(Three longer score notes appear at the end of the glossary.)

avec fraîcheur et naïveté, with a feeling of freshness and simplicity

bien chanté et très dehors, bring out [the melody] with a strong singing tone
brillante, sparkling, showy

croisez, cross [one hand over the other]

en mesure, sans ralentir, in time, without slowing
et très soutenu, and very sustained

fantasque et très passionné, fantastic (whimsical) and very impassioned

lent et déclamé, slowly, in a declamatory manner

m[ain] d[roite], right hand
m[ain] g[auche], left hand

presque sans mesure, almost "out of time" (without a beat feeling)
pressez (un peu), rushed, moving forward (a little)

remouvement de valse, "repetitious" waltz time [see the introduction, p. x]

sec, dry, staccato
sans presser, unrushed
sans ralentir (jusqu'à la fin), without slowing (until the end)

très calme, very calm
très doux, very gently
très en mesure, in strict time
très expressif, very expressive
très léger, very light
très rude, very rough, impetuous

un peu retenu, slightly held back

Longer Score Notes

Habanera, p. 87, footnote:
> *Pour faciliter la lecture de cette transcription, l'Auteur a divisé en deux portées la partie de la main gauche.*
> To simplify reading this transcription, the composer has notated the part for left hand on two staves.

Feuillet d'album, p. 103, main tempo:
> *en un mouvement assez lent de Valse, et très tendrement*
> in a rather slow waltz tempo, and very tenderly

Joyeuse marche, p. 114, 3rd system, l.h.:
> *écraser cet accord avec la* paume *de la main gauche*
> strike ["crush"] this chord with the *palm* of the left hand

Bourrée fantasque, p. 117, main tempo:
> *Très animé et avec beaucoup d'entrain*
> Very lively and with a great deal of spirit

INTRODUCTION

by Roy Howat

(Footnote commentaries appear at the end of the Introduction.)

More than anyone else of his century, Emmanuel Chabrier (1841–1894) restored to French music the essential French traits of clarity, emotional vitality, wit and tenderness, at a crucial time when the music of his country was struggling under a Wagnerian hangover on the one hand and academic dryness on the other. Chabrier's achievement is all the more remarkable in view of his own veneration for Wagner—though he was equally capable of lampooning his idol, as he did uproariously in his piano duet *Souvenirs de Munich*.

Ironically, we have Wagner to thank for setting this musical revolution irreversibly on course. It was a visit to Munich in 1880, to hear *Tristan und Isolde*, that finally prompted Chabrier to abandon his post at the Ministry of the Interior (where for almost twenty years he had amused his colleagues and occasionally exasperated his superiors), and devote all his remaining time to music. His decision was timely, for only eleven years of full-time composition and performance remained before a nervous paralysis (of syphilitic origin) made creative work impossible for the last three years of his life.

Like Fauré and Ravel, Chabrier was a countryman by birth, one who liked to affirm that "my music rings with the stamp of my Auvergnat clogs." The pianos that emerged with broken strings and hammers from Chabrier's famous solo renditions of *España* would probably have agreed about the clogs. But that is only part of the story: his friend Vincent d'Indy later described Chabrier as a pianist whose brilliance, delicacy and range of color he had never heard surpassed "except perhaps by Liszt and Anton Rubinstein." Chabrier's Auvergnat clogs show themselves most clearly in the fast stamping rhythms that pervade works like *Bourrée fantasque*, *Joyeuse marche*, *Danse villageoise*, *Menuet pompeux*, the central part of *Paysage* and even *España*.

From his early twenties, Chabrier was embroiled in the Parisian avant-garde, becoming a close friend of Verlaine, Monet, Renoir, Sargent and Manet (who died in Chabrier's arms). His collection of Impressionist paintings, built up long before the painters became famous, was one of the finest ever in private hands (Manet's "Un bar aux Folies-Bergère" hung above the composer's piano). In 1877, the success of his comic opera *L'étoile* first established his reputation, three years before he resigned his office job and six years before *España* took Paris by storm.

Chabrier's short but brightly burning career left us a song output equal in quantity and quality to Duparc's, a piano output almost as large as Ravel's, and a glittering array of choral and orchestral showpieces, including operatic numbers that range from sidesplitting comedy to almost (but never quite) Wagnerian grandeur. His brilliant orchestration—which he claimed he learned by copying out at least part of *Tannhäuser*—was unique and virtually infallible, despite the huge risks it often took. He knew musical history minutely, and how to prune all unnecessary detail from his music—a quality that must have endeared him to Ravel, that archenemy of musical padding. A rotund, extroverted man of wide erudition, Chabrier liked to describe himself as "the least illiterate of musicians," and his rustic spontaneity disguised much hard work and quiet professionalism, accompanied by a razor wit that quickly punctured any condescension: Benjamin Godard once foolishly told him, "What a pity, *mon cher* Emmanuel, that you took up music so late," only to wilt under the retort, "An even greater pity, *mon cher* Benjamin, that you took it up so early."

Chabrier's musical expression, matching his boisterous yet sensitive personality, ranges from sheer buffoonery to the utmost tenderness, often taken skillfully to the very edge of sentiment. This sometimes earned him accusations of vulgarity (including a rabid denunciation from Cosima Wagner), though Ravel later derided such charges as "an odd defect to find in a musician whose imprint can be identified in any three bars of his work."

Indeed, Ravel declared that he would rather have written Chabrier's *Le roi malgré lui* than the whole of Wagner's *Ring*, and he repeatedly named Chabrier as the composer who had influenced him more than any other. The young Debussy for his part was reduced to tears of helpless mirth by the "Chartreuse verte" duet from *L'étoile*. In 1886, he played Chabrier's two-piano *Valses romantiques* to Liszt, and as late as 1913 he tricked his conductor friend Inghelbrecht into repeating Chabrier's *Ode à la musique* during valuable rehearsal time, just for the pleasure of hearing "such a beautiful" work twice. Manuel de Falla admired the skill with which Chabrier carried Andalusian music into *España*, and even Stravinsky quotes from Chabrier's music, as did César Franck while Chabrier was still alive. Francis Poulenc, in a delightfully affectionate book about Chabrier, declared the *Pièces pittoresques* to be "as important for French music as Debussy's *Preludes*."[1]

Despite such acclaim, in his own time and after, even his

publishers found Chabrier's music "too complicated and difficult," and let some of his finest songs and piano music lie unpublished until after his death. Perhaps it is no surprise, then, that in the century following the composer's death even music lovers well acquainted with his immensely popular *España* and *Joyeuse marche* remain unfamiliar with the rest of his work.

This edition of the important solo piano music of Chabrier's mature years was inspired by the centennial, in 1994, of the composer's death, and is supported by research and insights generated by that anniversary. In addition, the recent publication of Chabrier's complete correspondence allows a more detailed chronology of his life and works than was hitherto possible. This is the source for all the following quotations from his letters.[2]

In addition to the twenty works in the present collection, numerous items of juvenilia survive, notably a *Marche des Cipayes* ("March of the Sepoys," originally composed in his schooldays as "*Le Scalp!!!*"), which was in print for most of Chabrier's life. One early piece on the borderline of his maturity, not included here, is *Air de ballet*, published posthumously in 1897. Although it has sometimes been ascribed to the 1870s, its style suggests more the early 1860s. An undated *Suite de valses*, published in 1913, is actually a piano reduction by an anonymous editor of a "short score" intended for orchestration. Of thirty-four apparently complete *Petits morceaux faciles* (Little easy pieces), no trace remains, alas, except for a surviving contents list in Chabrier's hand.[3]

Some unfinished pieces remain from Chabrier's mature years, including a large-scale *Capriccio*, a major work begun in 1883 and published in 1914 in a completion by Maurice Le Boucher (Editions Costallat, now Billaudot). Unfortunately its manuscript is lost, and the edition does not indicate where Le Boucher's completion takes over. (In 1960, Le Boucher wrote to Roger Delage that his contribution involved approximately the second half of the piece.) Although Chabrier was famous for his solo renditions of *España*, he left no written version in that form. He did, however, leave a scintillating two-piano version and an equally virtuoso piano part to his adaptation of *España* as a solo song; however, most editions of this song print the piano part in a simplified version. A less pianistic solo arrangement was written by Chabrier's colleague Camille Chevillard.

NOTES ON THE MUSIC

The lively, sophisticated **Impromptu**, first published in 1873, was given its concert premiere in 1877 by Camille Saint-Saëns. According to Chabrier's recollections in 1893 (in letters to Henri Heugel), it was composed in either 1865 or 1868. The piece's influence can be heard especially at the climax of Ravel's *Valses nobles et sentimentales*, and at the close of Debussy's prelude "La terasse des audiences du clair de lune" of forty years later.

Ronde champêtre (the title is not Chabrier's) was the second piece in an early draft of the *Pièces pittoresques*; it probably dates from the 1870s, perhaps earlier. Chabrier's publisher turned it down, and its printing was delayed until 1897.[4] Its main theme comes from the "Air de Poussah" ("Poussah's song") in a comic operetta Chabrier wrote with Paul Verlaine around 1864, a piece of chinoiserie cheekily entitled *Fisch-Ton-Kan*.[5]

Petite valse hides a humorous prank, as can be found by trying to end the piece! This little gem was written by Chabrier into the visitors' book of a restaurateur near the Normandy seaside town of Étretat on 26 June 1878. Its heading, "*Remouvement de valse*," puns not only in its hermetic repetitions but also on the fact that it follows a "*Mouvement de valse*" written into the same book by Chabrier's friend Edouard Moullé.[6] The opening is identical with the incipit for the eleventh of the lost *Petits morceaux faciles*, a two-page manuscript *Valse*. *Petite valse* (the title is not Chabrier's) is reproduced here from its only previous publication in the *Revue de Musicologie* of 1968, by kind authorization of the Société Française de Musicologie.

Over the summer of 1880, while on seaside vacation at Saint-Pair, Chabrier assembled the **Pièces pittoresques**. From letters to his publishers we learn that he initially planned a set of twelve pieces. As it was, he had to argue to have even the present ten accepted, including—almost incredibly—the ravishing "Idylle": his publisher Costallat blandly wrote to him on 26 July 1880, "we do not understand this piece." Thirty years later, the adolescent Francis Poulenc responded very differently on hearing "Idylle" from a sort of early juke box outside the Pathé record store in Paris. Half a century after the event, he recalled: "Today I still tremble with emotion thinking of the miracle that happened then; a new harmonic world opened up before me, and my own music has never forgotten that first *baiser d'amour*." In 1881, after the first performance of some of the *Pièces pittoresques*, César Franck remarked, "We have just heard something extraordinary: this music links our time with that of Couperin and Rameau."

"Idylle," Chabrier told his publisher Costallat, was inspired by a passage from "Senior est Junior," one of Victor Hugo's *Chansons des rues et des bois*.[7] (That same summer Chabrier set another poem from that collection, "Sommation irrespectueuse," as a song.) Chabrier was often haphazard about titles. While an autograph fragment of "Mauresque" shows its title in Chabrier's hand, his letters reveal that most of the other titles were added just before publication, with the help of his publisher and his friend Paul Lacome. (He may have been amused that the title "Improvisation" disguises the only strict sonata form in his whole output.) In 1888, Chabrier orchestrated "Idylle," "Danse villageoise,"

"Sous bois" and "Scherzo-valse" as *Suite Pastorale*. Ravel, who later made a magnificent orchestration of "Menuet pompeux," was also especially fond of "Sous bois," "Mauresque" and "Mélancolie," the last of which he considered very close in mood to Manet's painting *Olympia*.

Aubade was completed in February 1883, one of the first fruits of Chabrier's four-month visit to Spain in autumn 1882; a few of its turns of phrase anticipate *España*. Why this entrancing piece lay unpublished during Chabrier's life is unknown. *Habanera* followed in 1885; as with *España*, its themes come from music Chabrier heard in Spain. Chabrier orchestrated *Habanera* in 1888, adding nuances and harmonic retouches that were never carried over to the piano version; they are listed below, in the section headed *Sources and Variants*.

Ballabile and **Caprice**—the titles are possibly not Chabrier's—were probably composed together, since sketches for both occur on the same sheet of paper. Unpublished during Chabrier's lifetime, they may have been the two sightreading test pieces Chabrier provided in July 1889 for the Bordeaux Conservatoire. Besides its audible homage to *Tristan und Isolde*, *Caprice* carries clear echos of Mussorgsky's song "On the river" (from the cycle *Sunless*, published in 1874), notably its final bass ostinato. Another bass ostinato from the same song recurs in the last part of "Sous bois."

Feuillet d'album appeared in the art supplement of an unidentified magazine around 1890 (a poem on the preceding page is dated February 1890), surrounded and adorned with Art Nouveau figurations by Paul Steck. It is doubtless this piece that Chabrier describes in an undated letter: "It's a tender leaf of music . . . just some little daisies. A very pale fair-haired young girl, dreamy and compassionate." Since *Ballabile*, *Caprice* and *Feuillet d'album* are all ingeniously built around the same three-note melodic motive, they may well have been intended as a group.

Joyeuse marche began life in summer 1883 as a *Rondo* for piano duet, preceded by a *Prélude* which later became the orchestral *Prélude pastoral*. In 1885, Chabrier revised the two duets, renaming the second one *Marche française*. They lay neglected until 1888, when Chabrier orchestrated them for a concert of his works he conducted at Angers (the same concert for which he orchestrated *Suite pastorale* and *Habanera*). The success of the *Marche*—which, Chabrier wrote to his wife, had the orchestra "in stitches"—at last prompted Enoch & Costallat to publish it, renamed *Joyeuse marche*. In 1890, Chabrier produced the present piano solo version as well as a new arrangement for piano duet. Both piano versions of 1890 employ the same exuberant bass whack

using the whole hand (a cymbal blow in the orchestral score).

The **Bourrée fantasque**, Chabrier's last instrumental work, celebrates the *bourrée d'Auvergne*, a vigorous clog dance already heard in the central part of "Paysage." It is dedicated to the 18-year-old piano virtuoso Edouard Risler, to whom Chabrier wrote on 12 May 1891:

> "My dear young colleague, I've concocted a little piano piece for you which I think is quite fun and in which I've counted nearly 113 different sonorities. You'll see how luminously you make this one sparkle! It needs to sound wild and crazy!"

Had Chabrier's failing health not prevented him from completing its orchestration, it would doubtless have become an Auvergnat equivalent to *España* in the orchestral repertoire.

CHABRIER'S TEMPOS

The present volume reprints the most accurate original editions, with essential corrections taken from other sources as listed below. Editorial ties and hairpin dynamics are printed ⌒ and ⋗; other editorial additions are in square brackets. [ ].

A recurring problem concerns Chabrier's metronomic indications, many of which are implausibly fast (see table below). Those few indications which do make sense emphasize the problem with the others. For example, Chabrier's convincing indications for *Joyeuse marche* and *España* (giving a near-identity of sixteenth-note tempo across the two pieces) obviously bear on *Bourrée fantasque* (whose first five notes come verbatim from *España*, in addition to the clog stamp it shares with the opening of *Joyeuse marche*). This accords with the juxtaposed instructions "*Istesso tempo*" and "*Molto espressivo*" on the third page of *Bourrée fantasque*. In any case, the articulation marked in Chabrier's orchestrations of "Danse villageoise" and *Bourrée fantasque* necessitate more moderate tempi, and indeed Chabrier's orchestral scores of *Suite pastorale* and *Bourrée fantasque* omit the metronomic indications. It may simply be that Chabrier marked some indications away from the piano, or that one of his metronomes was inaccurate.[8] The implausible indications—included in the table below—have been removed in this edition.

Finally, Chabrier wanted his music vividly colored and dancelike, and, like most French composers, played basically in time, without *rallentando* or *rubato* except where indicated. It is worth noting that his instruction "*rit.*" sometimes applies to only a few expressive notes within a phrase, without his bothering to indicate the following return to *tempo*.

Title	Chabrier's indication	Editorial suggestion
Paysage	♩ = 132 (opening)	♩ = 120–126
	♩ = 160 (p. 21)	♩ = 138–144
Mélancolie	♪ = 80	♪ = 80
Tourbillon	♩. = 63	♩. = 63–56
Sous bois	♩ = 60	♩ = 60–66
Mauresque	♩ = 80	♩ = 72
Idylle	♩ = 120	♩ = 120
Danse villageoise	♩ = 160	♩ = 138–132
Menuet pompeux	♩ = 144 (opening)	♩ = 132–138
	♩ = 112 (p. 65)	♩ = 96
Joyeuse marche	♩ = 126	♩ = 126
Bourrée fantasque	♩ = 152	♩ = 132–138
(*España*	♩. = 80	♩. = 80)

SOURCES AND VARIANTS

Bar references are by page/system/bar (disregarding metrically incomplete opening bars).

Impromptu (pp. 1–8)

E1: first edition, Georges Hartmann, Paris, 1873, titled *1er Impromptu*. In 1891, Hartmann's catalogue was taken over by Henri Heugel, who planned to republish *Impromptu* in 1893; for reasons unknown this did not happen.

E2 (reproduced here): edition by Enoch, Paris, n.d.; anonymously revised by Gustave Samazeuil, whose annotated copy of E1 is in the archives of Enoch & Cie, Paris.

Text comments: E1 has too many misprints and omissions to be reproducible here, and no space for many essential accidentals. Several indications from E1, missing in E2, are tacitly restored here. Added ties and accidentals in E2, and corrections of misprints from E1, are tacitly retained when supported by parallel passages in E1; other added ties are shown as editorial; some overediting in E2 is tacitly removed. 1/1/1: E2 prints *Allegretto*; E1 clearly has *All°*. 1/4/1: E1 has bass F, not D (but D at 2/2/4 and the parallel passages 4 pages later). 3/3/3: E1–2 have *Ped.* instead of pedal release, probably a misprint or slip of Chabrier's pen. 3/4/1: E1–2 indicate pedal an eighth-note later. 3/5/5: E1–2 print a dot under RH E♭. 4/2/6: E1 indicates *I° tempo bien* [*sic*] *moderato*. 4/2/7, /3/2, /3/4: E1–2 indicate pedal engagement an eighth-note later.

4/5/4–5/1/5: triplet indications and rests in E2 only. 5/2/3: E1–2 indicate pedal only at last grace note. 7/4/3 & /5/3: E1 gives bass G as eighth-note (no following rest at /4/3, same rests as E2 at /5/3). 8/1/4: E1–2 continue upper slur to 3rd beat. 8/2/5: E1–2 indicate pedal a bar later. 8/3/7: E1 has accent to F instead of hairpin diminuendo; E2 retains accent but ties F to F of previous bar (given a value dot and added downstem).

Ronde champêtre (pp. 9–16)

E: first edition, Enoch, 1897.

A: autograph used for engraving E (archives of Enoch & Cie, Paris). There is no title, just the heading "II." See also footnote 4, below.

Text comments: Slurs from single grace notes occur only in E. The present reprint tacitly retains articulation in E carried over from parallel passages in A, but removes other unsupported additions, notably a dedication to Louis Diémer, ♩ = 126 at 9/1/1, ♩ = 84 at 10/1/2, and numerous pedal indications. Phrasing from A is restored here where E changes it to match other passages (for example 10/1/2 & 5 relative to 6 bars later). 11/3/3: values as in A; E has an eighth-note chord and quarter-note rest. 16/3/3 onwards: present 3/4 is pencilled in A, non-autograph, likewise ♯ to 16/4/1 LH lower C; A omits every other ♯ to C in last three bars except to bass C of 16/3/3 and left-thumb C of 16/4/1; A also omits ♯ to final G of 16/4/1.

Petite valse (p. 17)

E: *Revue de Musicologie*, vol. 54 (1968), no. 2, pp. 245–6; derived from the autograph in a private collection, Normandy.

Text comments: 17/2/2: E prints 1st top note as F, not E.

Pièces pittoresques (pp. 18–76)

E1: first edition, single volume, by Litolff, Brunswick, together with Enoch & Costallat, Paris.

E2 (reproduced here): revised separate print of each piece, more spaciously and accurately engraved, Enoch & Costallat, 1891 onwards. The main musical changes affect "Mauresque," issued in 1891, which has added pedalling, revised dynamics and some reworking of textures. Eight of the remaining pieces, issued in 1894–5, have added or revised articulation and nuances; "Paysage" also removes a two-page repetition from its central episode. "Scherzo-valse" was reengraved for E2 only in the 1900s, but with no musical changes from E1.

A: autograph fair copy of "Sous bois," bar 50 to the end, double folio, crossed through in blue pencil (Bibliothè-que Nationale, Paris, Rés. Uma ms.25). This fragment was possibly discarded because it is followed on the same page by an unfinished march in D major, headed "IV"; since the paper is identical with that of the autograph of *Ronde champêtre* (headed "II"), we can deduce that "Sous bois" was "III" at that stage. (The unfinished march was perhaps replaced by "Tourbillon.") Bars 1–2 of "Mauresque" survive in another autograph (no variants from E1–2); see notes to *Aubade*, below.

O: *Suite pastorale*, orchestral score of "Idylle" (in F), "Danse villageoise," "Sous bois" and "Scherzo-valse"; Enoch, 1896.

Text comments: Obvious misprints or *lacunae* in E2 are tacitly corrected by reference to E1; any corrections taken from A or O are listed below. Since A has different dynamics, only essential corrections from there, or details corroborated by O, are carried over to the present edition.

Paysage (pp. 18–25)

19/2/6: E1 places *rit.* in middle of following bar (but reads as E2 at 23/6/5). 19/5/4–6: E1 phrases RH as at 24/3/4–6 (without staccato dots); E2 revision perhaps intended for latter passage, too. 20/2/2 & 24/6/4: E1 ends RH slur a note earlier on D♯; comparison with imitative LH suggests that this reading is perhaps correct, also for 3, 6 and 9 bars before (Chabrier's autograph slurs tend to be written overlong). 21/5/1–22/6/4: E1 prints repeat marks around this section. 23/2/1: E1–2 give LH chord a third lower as D♭/F; *cf.* 3–4 bars later and page 18. 25/2/6: E2 prints *p*, probably a misreading of the first letter of "Pressez" (printed lower-case bold italic in E1).

"Tourbillon" (pp. 28–31)

29/4/4: E1–2 place *mf* a quarter-note beat later.

"Sous bois" (pp. 32–7)

32/2/1–2, 2–3: RH cross-bar slurs in O only, likewise RH mid-bar slurs in 32/2/3 & /3/3, also 33/2/2 where E1–2 begin slur from grace-note G. 33/2/3: E1–2, but not O, have a grace-note pair F-G (as in 32/3/4) before 1st grace note D; latter was probably part of a later revision (*cf.* 32/3/4) supplanting the F-G. 33/2/3–4: RH cross-bar slur as in O; E1–2 end it a note earlier (*cf.* 32/3/4 & 36/1/1). 35/1/3 & /2/2: *p* & *pp* from A, supported by O, not in E1–2. 35/4/1–2: *legato e molto tranquillo* placed as in A: E1–2 begin it after the double-bar. 36/1/1: RH lower slur in A & O, not in E1–2; A ends it under 2nd C. 36/2/4 & 37/1/1: staccato dots and lower *sf* from A, supported by O, not in E1–2; A also carries RH slur over to following bar, but O does not. 36/4/3: O has *Ritenuto* for 2 bars. 37/1/2–3: ⟩ in A only; A also has ⟩ in 37/1/1, not supported by O, which has *crescendo*. 37/2/4: no grace notes in any source, but perhaps intended: E2 has an illogical flat to top A of 2nd RH chord, possibly a misreading of an intended grace note; A & O also omit grace notes 8 & 14 bars earlier (in A they appear only at 36/2/3, apparently added later). 37/3/2: *Meno mosso* according to O; E1–2 print *rit.* instead. 37/3/3 to /4/1: RH slurs as in A; E1–2 end the first slur a note earlier and then print a single slur from 37/4/1 to first note of /4/2 (*cf.* 2 bars earlier). 37/4/3–4: ⟨ as in A: E1–2 begin and end it a quarter-note earlier. 37/5/1: LH slur as in A: E1–2 start it from bass C. 37/5/4: *ppp* according to A, *pp* in E1–2 (*pppp* in O).

"Mauresque" (pp. 38–43)

39/1/1 & /4/1, 41/4/1: E1 has *sf*, not *f* & *mf* (E2 omits the lower *mf* at 41/4/1); although *f* for *sf* is a frequent misprint in Chabrier, the consistency in E2 here, plus the variant *mf*, suggest deliberate change. 39/1/3: E1 includes a lower E in beat 3, 1st RH chord. 39/5/1: ♮ to final D not in E2, applies by default in E1 where 2nd beat grace note is C not D♯.

"Idylle" (pp. 44–49)

44/2/2–3: E1 has *sf* ⟩ *p* also for LH, similarly *sf* at /3/3 and *p* at /4/4; not in E2 or O. 45/5/1: LH given here as in E1; E2 reads as 8 bars earlier; O corroborates E1 (with added embellishment). 46/4/3 & 5: E1–2 end RH slur on 4th note and print accent instead of hairpin diminuendo to 3rd beat; O confirms present phrasing and nuances, as on page 49. 47/4/3: E1–2 in beat 3 both show a RH eighth-note A immediately below top C♯ (instead of taking the eighth-note stem from C♯; probably a misprint (*cf.* 2 bars later and 3 pages earlier). 49/4/1: ♮ to RH 4th beat A according to O, not in E1–2; likewise /5/3 first staccato dot.

"Danse villageoise" (pp. 50–55)

50/3/4 and all similar bars: E2 places quarter-note accents on LH chords, E1 prints them between the staves (*cf.* next bar). 50/4/1: E1–2 print redundant *ff*. 52/4/8 & 53/5/5: *mf* placed as in O; E1–2 place it at the beginning of 52/5/1. 53/5/4: O omits *rit.*

"Improvisation" (pp. 56–61)

56/1/2: E1 has *sf* and accent to RH top F, but no dash and dot; E2 has only the dash and dot; *cf.* 60/1/2. 59/3/3: C in 2nd RH chord perhaps a misprint for A; *cf.* 2 bars earlier. 61/3/1–2: continuous slurs in both systems perhaps a misprint; *cf.* 4 pages earlier. 61/5/2: E1–2 lead upper RH slur to last chord of bar, lower RH slur in E2 only.

"Menuet pompeux" (pp. 62–68)

63/2/3 & 67/5/2: 6th LH chord possibly misprint for a 3rd lower; *cf.* 64/3/4 & 68/4/4. 68/6/1: E1–2 center hairpin swell between beats 2 & 3; *cf.* 4 pages earlier.

"Scherzo-valse" (pp. 69–76)

69/1/1 and similar: O has *sf* to B. 70/6/4: *f* according to O, not in E1–2. 71/2/1: O has *dolce* & *p* reverting to *f* at end of /4/4. 74/4/4–6 & /5/3–5: the present LH hairpins (as in E1–2) may be intended accents; O gives these chords in eighth-note pairs on beats 2–3, with accents on beat 2 at /4/4–6 but diminuendo hairpins at /5/3–5. 75/2/4–5, /3/3–4 & /4/2–3: O has *Riten. molto* over these bars. 75/5/2: O adds a bar's rest with pause before the *f* upbeat.

Aubade (pp. 77–86)

E: first edition, Enoch, 1897.

A: incomplete autograph, 4 pp., lacking a final page [84/5/2 onwards] (Musée de la Musique, Paris; bequeathed by Roger Désormière). Its original title, "Mazurka," is deleted and replaced in turn by "Intermezzo" and then "Sérénade," followed by a dedication "A Madame Etienne Pallu." At the bottom of the first page, Chabrier later pencilled: "Nota—Encore un qui ne sera pas de sitôt gravé" ["Note—Another one that won't be published in a hurry"]. The musical text is essentially that of E but with many variants of nuance and performing indications. The second autograph page, upside down, contains bars 1–2 of "Mauresque" with title, heavily deleted in ink.

Text comments: An autograph exhibited in 1941 (collection of Mme Bretton-Chabrier, now untraced) appears to have borne the present title and dedication as well as the date February 1883, suggesting that E was engraved from that and not from A above.[9] Only essential variants from A are therefore used or listed here: in particular, a few obviously misplaced nuances and slurs in E are tacitly corrected by reference to A. The following appear only in A: 78/1/3 & 79/2/3, *sf*; 78/3/2, *leggiero*; 79/5/1–3, staccato dots; 80/5/2 & 81/1/1, LH articulation; 80/5/3, beat 1 RH $>$ & lower slur; 81/1/3–2/1: *m.g.* indication & lower slur (leading to /2/2); 81/2/3–/3/3, RH $>$; 81/3/3–/4/2, each $>$; 81/5/3, upstem & value dot to 2nd penultimate LH A; 82/1/4, *espressivo* & slur; 82/5/2, 2nd accent; 82/5/3, *riten.*; 83/1/1 & 1st chord of /1/2, LH articulation (A continues accents to 1st chord of /2/1); 83/2/1–2, *riten.*, *Pressez* & LH tenuti; 83/3/1 & 2, LH *sf* (replacing staccato dot in E); 83/3/3, *rit. poco*; 83/4/3, staccato dots. 77/1/1: A has tempo heading "(*Allegro non tanto*)" and omits tempo changes on pp. 78 & 79. 77/2/2: RH accents as in A; E follows LH articulation (*cf.* pages 80 & 86). 80/4/1–82/3/3: A sometimes arpeggiates different

chords from E. 81/2/1: A centers hairpin swell at beat 2. 83/1/1–/2/2: E prints *a Tempo* at beat 1 of 83/1/1 & /2/1, and *rit.* at last eighth-note of /2/2; their relative redundancy suggests they may have been editorial additions to counter E's lack of some of the surrounding indications. 83/2/2: A gives 1st RH note as sixteenth-note B, not eighth-note C♯, and omits rests. 84/3/3–/4/1: upper slurs not in A, should perhaps read as on p. 78. 86/1/1 & 3: E centers hairpin swell on 4th eighth-note of bar. 86/4/4: E prints bottom note of 1st RH chord as F♯, not E, probably misprint (*cf.* 77/2/1 & 80/3/2).

Habanera (pp. 87–93)

E: first edition, Enoch & Costallat, 1885.

O: orchestral score (in D), Enoch & Costallat, 1889.

Text comments: O gives the following variant tempo indications: 89/2/4, *Poco più mosso*; 90/1/4, *Riten*; 90/2/2, *Tranquillo*; 90/4/2, *Più mosso*; 91/3/2, *Ritard.*; 91/4/2, *Ritard. poco* (for 2 bars); 92/2/1, *Meno mosso*; 92/3/4, *Risoluto*, *f* on anacrusis to half bar. 90/1/4–/2/1: O adds the following arpeggio in the strings (transposed here):

90/4/1: O has *sf* on 2nd chord. 91/3/1, top staff: from 2nd eighth-note onward, O repeats the harmony of 4 bars earlier, an octave lower. 91/3/2: O has 1st melody note a tone higher (F here instead of E♭), similarly at 93/2/4 (B♭ instead of A♭). 92/2/2–4: O gives counter-melody's rhythm and dynamics (cellos) as

93/3/3–/4/2: O modifies harmony and texture; piano reduction equivalent is:

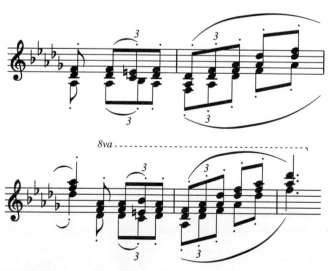

Ballabile (pp. 94–98)

E: first edition, Enoch, 1897.

A: autograph draft (collection of Thierry Bodin, Paris), lacking only the 4 silent bars and 97/1/5 to /2/2; the last bar is followed by a sketch of the last 7½ bars of *Caprice*. No titles appear.

Text comments: 97/1/5: E ends ◁ before barline (this bar not in A). 97/4/2: pedal release sign as in A: E places it after beat 3.

Caprice (pp. 99–102)
E: first edition, Enoch, 1897. The autograph sketch (see *Ballabile* above) yields no corrections here.

Text comments: 100/1/1 & 3, 102/1/1 & /2/1–2: E continues each ◁ almost to beat 3. 100/1/2: E prints *f* above tied beat 3, then *sf* above following quarter-note E♯. 101/3/2 onwards: E prints additional slurs inconsistently across some or part of the triplet groups, probably a misreading of triplet brackets, removed here. 102/1/2: E leads RH upper slur to beat 1 A♯ instead of F♯.

Feuillet d'album (pp. 103–106)
F: feuilleton publication in the musical supplement of an unidentified journal (Bibliothèque Nationale, Paris, Gr. Uma 138).

E (reproduced here): edition by Enoch, 1897. It is not known if E was prepared from F or from an autograph.

Text comments: E adds a dedication to Edouard Risler (at Risler's request to Chabrier's widow), and "♩ = 138" preceding the tempo heading; the position of the latter suggests it was added in a proof. The following appear only in F: 103/1/1, *pp* to LH; 104/1/3, bass value dot; 104/2/1–2, LH rest & upper LH cross-bar slur; 104/2/3, LH dot & dash; 105/2/3, 1st staccato dot; 105/3/2, slur across staves; 106/1/2–3, F♯-F♯ tie; 106/4/2, upper *ppp*. 104/1/4: F has RH *pp*, not *p*, and a value dot to the bass, but omits *dim.*, slur from bass & E from beat 3 LH chord. 104/3/2: F slurs both hands from beat 1 C♯ to beat 3 E, then new slurs from next bar D♯. 106/2/1–2: F has single bass slur (A-F♯) instead of 2 separate slurs.

Joyeuse marche (pp. 107–116)
ES: first edition for piano solo, Enoch & Costallat, 1890.
ED: first edition for piano duet, Enoch & Costallat, 1890.
O: orchestral score, Enoch & Costallat, 1890.

Text comments: Obvious misprints or omissions of essential details are tacitly corrected by reference to ED. 107/1/1: metronomic indication present only in ED; O has *Tempo di marcia, molto risoluto e giocoso.* 109/3/3: *mf* in ED only.

Bourrée fantasque (pp. 117–128)
E: first edition, Enoch & Costallat, 1891.
A: autograph used for engraving the first edition (Bibliothèque Nationale, Paris, Ms. 19201).
O: unfinished autograph orchestral score, up to 6/2/2 (Bibliothèque Nationale, Paris, Ms. 20622).

Text comments: Some inexact placing of nuances and pedalling in E is tacitly corrected by reference to A. Essential nuances, articulation and pedalling that appear only in A are tacitly incorporated here, except in cases where E

shows revised nuances. O: tempo heading is *Vivo.* 117/1/1: A indicates *staccatissimo*, not *marcatissimo*; the latter could be a misreading in E, though *cf. sempre marcato* at 118/2/3. 118/1/4: A omits grace note, implying its similar addition at 125/5/5 (as given here editorially); likewise 128/3/6 relative to 8 bars later. 118/4/1, 124/4/2: RH quarter-note rest in A only, indicating beat 2 as a different voice; O gives beat 1 to violas (*f*), beat 2 to 1st violins (*ff*). 119/5/5: ◁ *sf* ▷ present in A & O but not E; A (but not O) also has *sf* below last LH chord, and places *molto espressivo* 2 bars earlier. 120/1/5: A phrases RH G to E, then new phrase from next bar. 120/3/2: A has *sf* on 2nd LH chord, not in O. 120/4/7: O has

120/5/6–7: O centers hairpin swell at beginning of 120/5/7 (rising line in violins), then has ◁ across 121/1/2–3 (woodwind). 121/3/2: *Poco acceler.* placed as in A; E prints it a bar later. 121/3/3: A ties last 2 RH chords. 123/1/6 to /2/1: A omits lower RH slur completion in /2/1, otherwise phrases as here; E slurs D♯ in each hand to following E, then similarly G to F. 123/5/4: A has *rit. assai.* 124/2/1: A has *pp* in the bass; *ppp* in E is possibly a confusion with next bar? 124/2/2: A places final ▷ an eighth-note later (in next bar). 126/1/2–3: E prints *dimin.* ▷ from start of /1/2 to center of /1/3, omitting slur in /1/2. 127/3/3: E has accent under RH tied C; A has dot and dash instead, with no tie. 127/6/1: A delays pedal release until last note of next bar.

NOTES

[1] Francis Poulenc, *Emmanuel Chabrier* (Geneva & Paris, La Palatine, 1961; English translation by Cynthia Jolly, London, Dennis Dobson, 1981).

[2] *Emmanuel Chabrier, Correspondance,* ed. Roger Delage, Frans Durif & Thierry Bodin (Paris, Klincksieck, 1994). For pictorial and other documentation of Chabrier's life, see Roger Delage, *Emmanuel Chabrier, Iconographie musicale* (Paris, Minkoff & Lattès, 1982).

[3] The undated list, with musical incipits, titles and page numbers, is in a private collection in France. Three incipits relate to known works by Chabrier, including two operatic arias.

[4] The top of the manuscript has the pencilled comment "ajourni" ["laid aside"], followed by a note in Chabrier's hand: "écriture de Costallat. Il a dit: *caca* à ce morceau. A cette époque là, il commençait à rechigner sur tout. Ils en ont pourtant payé de moins chouettes que celui-ci." ["Costallat's writing. *Crap,* he said to this piece. At that time he was starting to balk at everything. Yet they bought less pretty pieces than this."]

[5] A pun on a vulgar French expletive.

[6] For a full commentary on this piece see François Durif, "Petite valse inédite d'Emmanuel Chabrier," *Revue de Musicologie,* vol. 54 (1968), no. 2, pp. 245–8.

[7] "Je vis aux champs, j'aime et je rêve / Je suis bucolique et berger / Je dédie aux dents blanches d'Ève / Tous les pommiers de mon verger." [I live in the country, I love and dream; I am a rustic and a shepherd; I dedicate to Eve's white teeth all the apple trees in my orchard.]

[8] Poulenc's declaration (*op. cit.*) that Chabrier's metronomic indications "*are all correct*" cannot be taken literally in every case, though it is a timely warning against sluggish tempos in this music. Poulenc also usefully recommends ♪ = 192 (Ricardo Viñes's tempo) for "Scherzo-valse."

[9] *Exposition Emmanuel Chabrier, Théâtre National de l'Opéra-Comique du 18 Janvier au 16 Février 1941, Catalogue rédigé par Auguste Martin* (Paris, 1941), p. 23, item 100.

To Madame Édouard Manet

IMPROMPTU

[To Louis Diémer]

RONDE CHAMPÊTRE
(Rustic round)

Animato e leggieramente.

dolce.

con delicatezza.

ritenuto.

PETITE VALSE

(Little waltz)

Remouvement de valse
(Libidino soudente)

PIÈCES PITTORESQUES

(Picturesque pieces)

To Madame the Countess de Narbonne-Lara

PAYSAGE

(Landscape)

Pièce Pittoresque No. 1

To Madame Marie Pillon

MÉLANCOLIE
(Melancholy)

Pièce Pittoresque No. 2

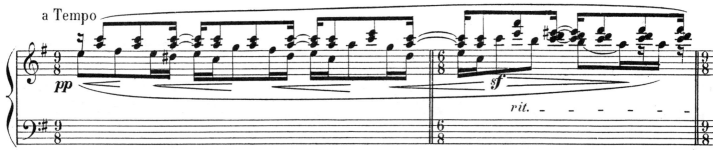

To Madame Marie Meurice

TOURBILLON
(Whirlwind)

Pièce Pittoresque No. 3

To Mademoiselle Marie de la Guéronnière

SOUS BOIS
(In the woods)

Pièce Pittoresque No. 4

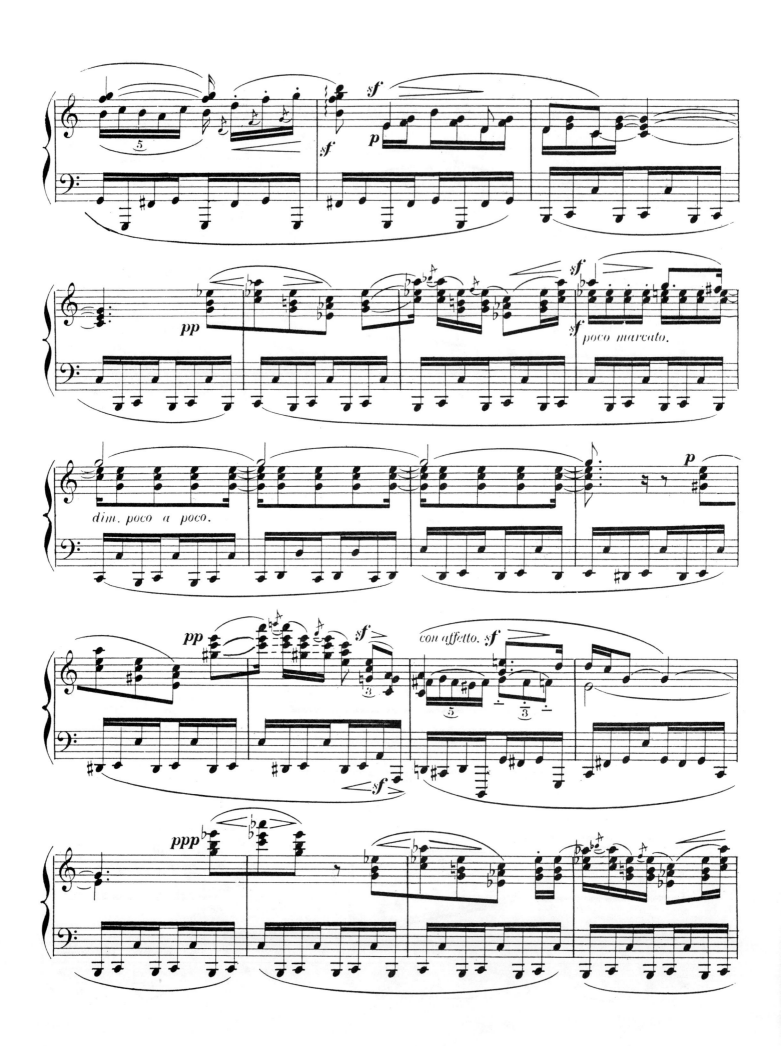

To Madame Charles Phalen

MAURESQUE
(In Moorish style)

Pièce Pittoresque No. 5

To Mademoiselle Jane Monvoisin

IDYLLE
(Idyll)

Pièce Pittoresque No. 6

To *Mademoiselle Yvonne de Montesquieu*

DANSE VILLAGEOISE

(Village dance)

Pièce Pittoresque No. 7

54   *Danse villageoise*

IMPROVISATION

Pièce Pittoresque No. 8

Ben moderato

To Mademoiselle Gabrielle Petitdemange

MENUET POMPEUX
(Festive minuet)

Pièce Pittoresque No. 9

Allegro franco.

Meno mosso e molto dolce e grazioso.

To Mademoiselle Mina de Gabriac

SCHERZO-VALSE
(Scherzo-waltz)

Pièce Pittoresque No. 10

AUBADE
(Dawn serenade)

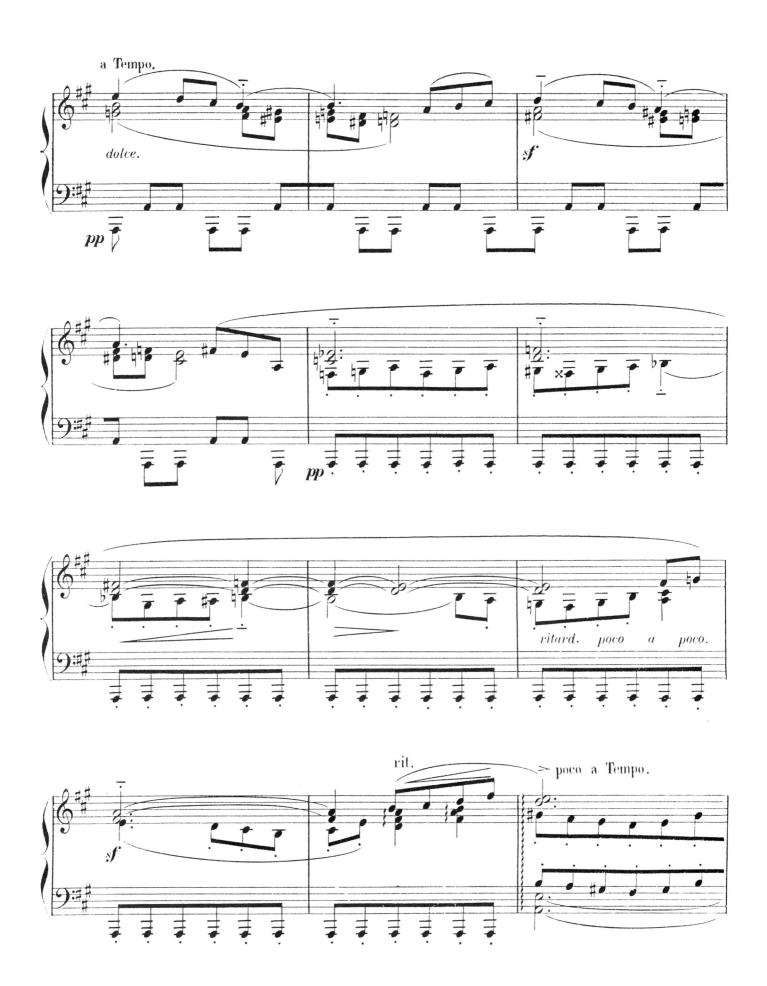

To Mademoiselle Marguerite Lamoureux

HABANERA

Transcribed for piano by the composer

Pour faciliter la lecture de cette transcription, l'Auteur a divisé en deux portées la partie de la main gauche.

BALLABILE
(Dancelike)

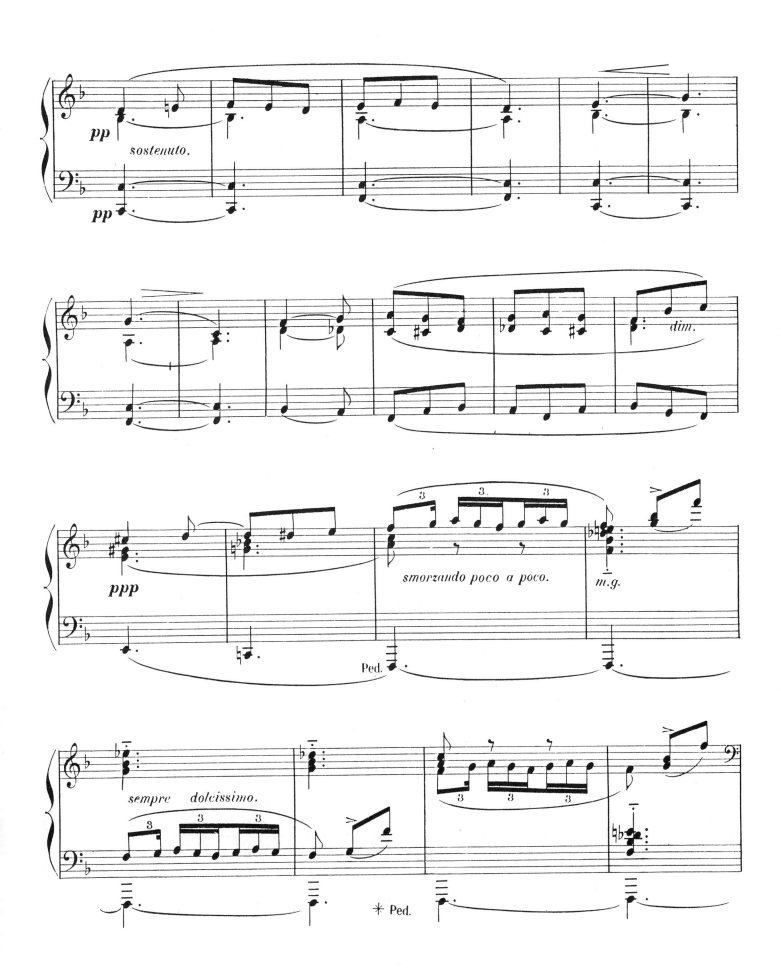

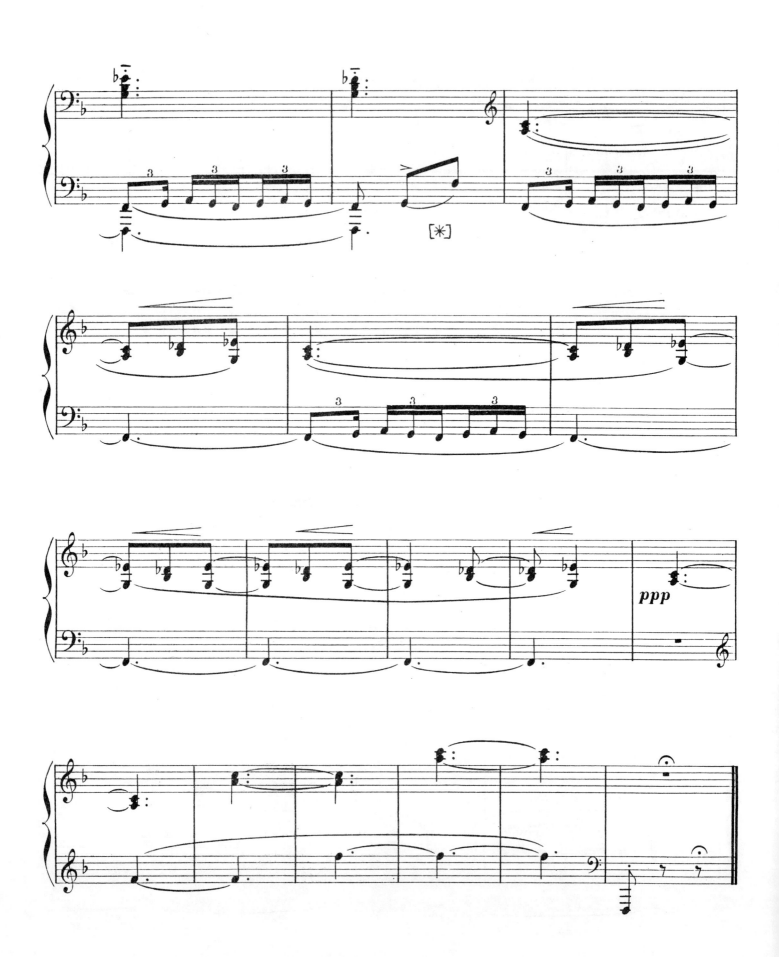

CAPRICE

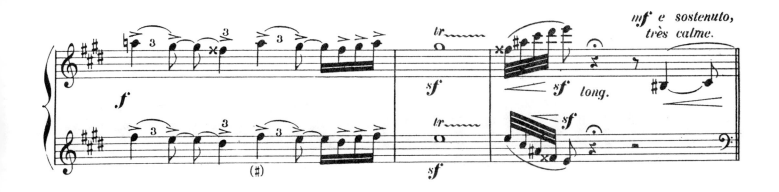

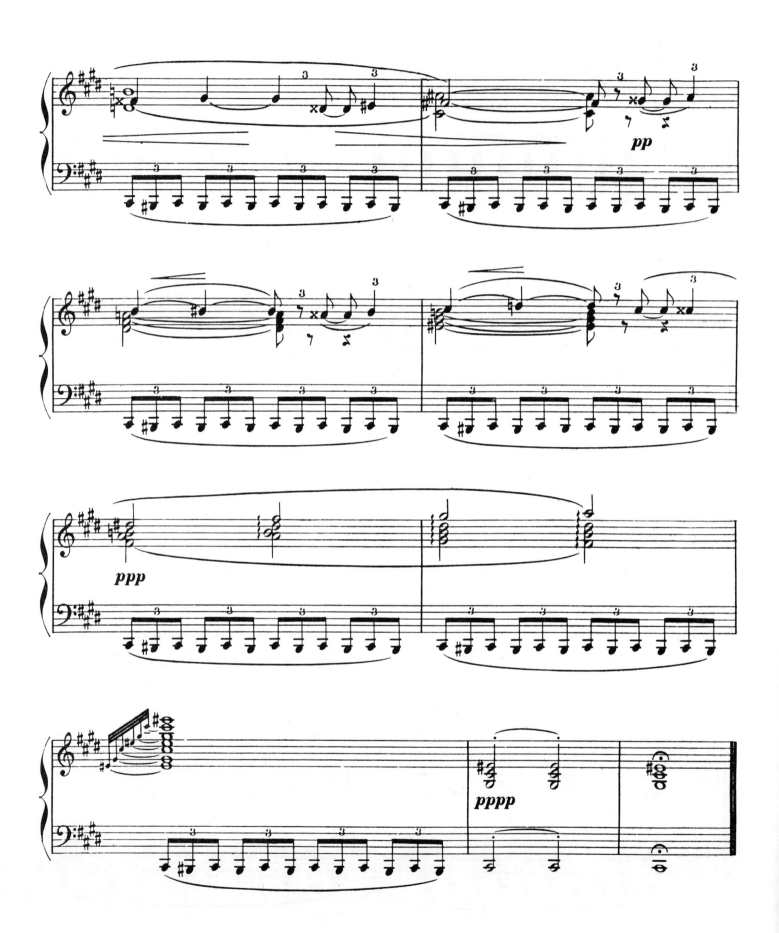

FEUILLET d'ALBUM
(Albumleaf)

En un mouvement assez lent de Valse, et très tendrement.

JOYEUSE MARCHE
(Joyous march)

fff 8ª bassa écraser cet accord
avec la *paume* de la main gauche.

To Édouard Risler

BOURRÉE FANTASQUE
(Fantastic bourrée)

Très animé et avec beaucoup d'entrain.

117

Bourrée fantasque

sempre molto risoluto.

pp

crescendo.

END OF EDITION